PRODUCTION ALGEBRA

A Handbook for Production Assistants

By Mark Adler
Michigan Production Alliance

FERNE PRESS

Production Algebra: A Training Manual for Production Assistants
Copyright © 2009 by Mark Adler
Printed in Canada

Summary: An instruction manual for those looking to enter the filming and production job market at the production assistant level.

Library of Congress Cataloging-in-Publication Data
  Adler, Mark
  Production Bootcamp / Mark Adler – First Edition
  ISBN-13: 978-1-933916-40-8
  1. Film and Video 2. Occupations 3. Production industry
  4. Production assistants
  I. Adler, Mark II. Production Bootcamp
  Library of Congress Control Number: 2009927976

All photos by Mark Adler.

FERNE PRESS

Ferne Press is an imprint of Nelson Publishing & Marketing
366 Welch Road, Northville, MI 48167
www.nelsonpublishingandmarketing.com
(248) 735-0418

CONTENTS

Dedication v

Introduction vii

Chapter 1: What Is a Production Assistant? 1

Chapter 2: On Set Etiquette 11

Chapter 3 : Housekeeping and Other
Responsibilities On Set or Location 17

Chapter 4: A Day in the Life on the Set 25

Chapter 5: Pay Rates and Scheduling 31

Conclusion 35

Appendix 37

DEDICATION

This manual is dedicated to the teachers and mentors
that have helped me along the way,
and to my wife who supports me through it all.
Thanks to everyone.

INTRODUCTION

This manual is intended to give you a realistic and practical overview of how the film and video production industry works for entry-level workers. We have compiled information from our own experiences, as well as those from other professionals across the United States.

The first and most important thing to learn about the film industry in any city is that production is a team effort. From script to edit, the making of a motion picture, commercial, television show, or music video requires the collaboration of what may well be hundreds of people, from production crew to talent and extras.

If you want a career in this industry, strong organizational skills will come in handy. You'll have to be able to relate to a variety of different people, doing a variety of different jobs in many departments. While the atmosphere may appear casual, production sets are actually running based on time-tested methods that come from disciplines such as communication, quality control, safety, and efficiency. It is important that everyone who reports to set for the first time learns and adheres to these methods.

Additionally, you'll need to understand the distinction between two dynamics occurring on any production set: the business of production and the creative side. Production administration and Creative—the yin and yang of the industry, if you will—must work together for a successful project to happen. The algebra we allude to is here—finding the solution to issues that always appear.

Another consideration is that film and video production is hard work. Projects are a special sort of organized chaos which again constitutes the algebraic equation. Production crews work extremely long hours for days in a row and often in trying conditions. If shooting a music video sounds glamorous, consider working sixteen hours or more a day, night shoots, outside, and in inclement weather. A positive attitude is essential, and its importance cannot be overstated. No matter how technically skilled a person is, a poor attitude can derail a film career very quickly. On the other hand, an upbeat, hardworking, and respectful person who is willing to learn has great potential to move up the ladder quickly.

This manual will help get you started as a freelance production professional. But you'll find that you must follow up with a wide variety of seminars, web-based information, trade magazines, networking, and membership in guilds, unions, or trade organizations to keep sharp and competitive.

At any level, even as a Production Assistant (P.A.), which is our focus here, the more you bring to the party (so to speak) in terms of ingenuity and determination, the more you will be the common denominator, which will serve you well.

"Vanities" working with talent

CHAPTER 1
WHAT IS A PRODUCTION ASSISTANT?

You're called a lot of things, which might include go-getter or gofer. A P.A. is a freelance, non-union position and usually the lowest paid, especially for the amount of work you will do. You will work either as a day player, that is, a person hired on a day-to-day basis, or for the "run of the show." You're inserted into the equation that is a particular job and assigned tasks to help move the production along.

Go for the chauffeur's endorsement on your driver's license for an edge ahead of others.

Job Description for a P.A.

- Have a valid driver license. Go for a chauffeur's endorsement for an edge ahead of others!
- Have a serviceable vehicle.
- Be knowledgeable of many geographic areas.
- Be knowledgeable of location of twenty-four hour facilities (hospitals too!).
- Must know how to use a phone book and online search engines.

- Expected to run at a moment's notice anywhere instructed, get there safely, keep production apprised of progress, and return quickly and successfully.
- Must be ready to paint studio floors.
- Must be ready to sweep floors or sidewalks, rake grass, cut branches, and move trash barrels.
- Must maintain stages or locations, taking care to keep all areas clean of cigarette butts and other human refuse.
- Have basic math skills, ability to balance a petty cash report, and the ability to handle large sums of cash.
- Make film runs and drops—both pickup and delivery (sometimes after hours)—as well as runs to an airport.
- Handle security, assigned to guard production equipment and/or "hot" locations or sets ("hot" refers to a working area).
- Set (studio or location) cleanup.
- First to come, last to leave.

A P.A.'s Kit

Every P.A. needs a kit. We'll discuss this in detail later in this manual, but here is a basic list:

- Pager, cell phone, or messaging device
- USB drive loaded with information you need to do the job
- Extra batteries (AA, AAA, watch battery type)
- Leatherman tool or Swiss Army knife
- Tape roll (gaffers and paper)
- Weather gear
- Clipboard or pad to write on (writing implement that works too)
- Tool kit—optional, as a Leatherman tool or Swiss Army knife does it all

- Screwdriver, razor knife, Sharpie marker
- Small first-aid kit
- Weather bag: a duffle or knapsack containing essential clothing

DNA OF P.A.s

The production industry is broad and varied in terms of why and where projects are produced. P.A.s fit into the equation because they help support all other departments. On large sets, you will usually work with a union crew consisting of a gaffer, grips, director of photography, script supervisor, camera assistants, and assistant directors. Other departments represented will include an art department, accounting, props, special effects, teamsters (who drive the vehicles), the "vanities" (hair, makeup, and wardrobe), video assist, sound, set decorations, and construction. On larger sets, you'll meet many P.A.s who are assigned responsibilities by department. On smaller sets, a single person will perform many jobs.

Making things safe on set is a key concern for a P.A.

As you continue reading, you'll find a breakdown of P.A. positions in these segments of the industry. Keep in mind that while some tasks can be viewed as menial, when you look at the big picture, a P.A. is considered the glue that holds the important parts of a job together.

CORPORATE SEGMENT

Corporations of a certain size may be able to afford either a production department or budgets for freelance assistance to create newsletters or updates for their clients, shareholders, or customers. A large corporation, like a pharmaceutical firm, might employ a producer who is allowed to hire small crews for such projects. A smaller corporation, like a tool and die maker, might have a public relations department that can contract for similar services.

In either scenario, a production assistant is often hired. A corporate P.A. position is an interesting starting point for an entry-level worker because it allows great flexibility in tasks. In a corporate setting, a P.A. might get coffee for the crew but may have also hired them and secured needed equipment.

Because of this flexibility, a corporate P.A. gains a great deal of specific knowledge which is of enough value that he or she might be hired for a long term. We, in the industry, have developed the name "permalancer" to describe this job category. Permalancer is an apt title as this person might work for months at a time for one client, performing tasks such as research or supervising an edit session. It can also lead to a full-time position, which is very good gig to have.

Corporate P.A. Snapshot:

- Daily hours, but not nine to five.
- Could be long term—hence the name "permalancer."
- Research multimedia libraries, assist producers in edits, hire crew, and rent equipment.
- Some travel involved.
- This work sometimes leads to a full-time position.

COMMERCIAL SEGMENT

A P.A. hired to work on a commercial is more of what the business refers to as a "day player." This position is hired on a day-to-day basis usually for prep, shoot, and wrap days depending on the length of the job.

A commercial P.A. has a bit less responsibility since most of the organizational work is performed by the production department, which consists of the Assistant Director (A.D.) and the Coordinator. The production department assigns tasks to the P.A., and it is common to have many workers in this position.

On some commercials, you might be driving a motor home or production cube van, in addition to helping lock down a set or street.

Commercial P.A. Snapshot:

- You will typically be hired for prep, shoot, and wrap days, and being the glue that holds the show together you will help out on the set. For example, you may page, or hold, a cable attached to a film or video camera. The set decorator might ask you to move set pieces or other equipment.

- You might be sent blocks away to hold both vehicle and human traffic or you might get coffee for the A.D. as well as refresh two-way radio batteries.

- Sometimes you will be given petty cash which you will use to make purchases for the project. You must keep track of all your receipts and be able to balance a petty cash report. You may also be asked to disburse this money, or per diems, to other crew members.

- In short, you'll do anything needed, as quickly and efficiently as possible.

FEATURES SEGMENT

On feature films, you will find a variety of P.A. backgrounds and experience. State film offices are asked for suggestions. Film schools and organizations also contribute and recommend names. Lower budgets and micro budget features are excellent training grounds for many crafts including P.A.s. Pay levels tend to be lower on features (commercials pay more) for P.A.s and other crew. Even workers will less training, fresh out of school, tend to find work. P.A.s are attached to the A.D. department, so developing relationships with A.D.s, as well as other P.A.s, is good policy. P.A.s with more experience might be attached to the set, to the A.D. Department, or are assigned to coordinate a staff of their own.

Features P.A. Snapshot:

- You are hired for the duration ("run of the show") of a feature or documentary project which could be three to six months, or as a "day player" on a day-to-day basis.

- On a feature, you could be a set P.A., be an office runner, get linked to a department like Casting, Wardrobe, or A.D., or you might assist with background, paperwork, and administration as an office P.A., or with more experience, an assistant production office coordinator (APOC).

- Locations P.A.s make sure the cast and crew members have such creature comforts as propane heaters in the cold and popup tents when it rains.

LIVE SHOWS SEGMENT

Many cities host live TV or event shows and require production personnel, which includes P.A.s. In this position, like a corporate P.A., there is a great deal of multitasking. These are live situations where tact and cleverness come in handy. As in all versions of this job, quick thinking, a way of remembering logistical information, and a good attitude make the job fun and earn you more opportunities.

Live Shows P.A. Snapshot:

- Hired in advance of the show (i.e. auto shows, X games).
- Assists producer in securing props, equipment, and talent.
- Responsible for paperwork, organizing information, and, in some cases, crew calls.
- In this scenario, this position also assists with crowd control.

"Crafty" is the heart of the show. They make sure everyone has the comfort foods that keep them going. This position can be as simple as buying bagels and coffee, or as complex as outfitting a cube van to serve breakfast and a late meal. Often this department is where P.A.s enter the industry, but in many cities the craft service people must have a wide range of experience.

Craft Service P.A. Snapshot:

- Dependent on the project, hired for prep, shoot, and sometimes wrap.
- Early and late hours.

Duties:

- Shopping—great fun or drudge, lots of shopping, loading carts with weird food items.
- Offer snack-type foods and sandwiches as well as specialty health drinks on set, discreetly and without distracting the crew.
- Must fill out petty cash reports and keep receipts.
- Must maintain food supplies for the term of the project and replenish within a specified budget.

Supplies:

- Basic needs: separate coolers for water and juice/soda pop and other beverages.
- Some craft service crew work out of vehicles. It's better to have a larger vehicle when you are secure in this position and can afford it.

SLATE PERSON

Occasionally, on a corporate or commercial set you may be asked to control the slate or clapper. This takes some housekeeping and organization. Basically, you communicate with the script person for scene and take numbers and the Camera Assistant (A.C.) for film speed and roll numbers. In most situations, the camera assistant or a loader will do this job as it is covered by the International Alliance of Theatrical and Stage Employees (IATSE) 600.

An example of a slate.

If you are asked to step in, your job is to keep track of this information on both the slate and sometimes on a camera report attached to the back of the slate. The Camera Assistant will instruct you on how he or she likes to mark the report...if they let you do that!

Once the A.D. calls for camera to roll, you stick the slate in, tilt towards a light so it can be captured properly, and if it is a sound take, call out the info on the slate. When working with professional talent, animals, or children you must use "quiet sticks." "Quiet sticks" is simply a softer clap so as not to startle or distract those in front of the camera. Sometimes, the camera will not be rolling (for a variety of reasons) when you clap the slate—in that case someone will then yell for "second sticks." Finally, if for any reason a "head" slate was not captured at the beginning of the take, a "tail", or end slate, will be requested. This slate would be captured upside down.

These are the basics, the areas where a production assistant might find work. Now let's delve a bit deeper into the etiquette and duties of this entry-level position.

Basic utility belt

Chapter 2
On Set Etiquette

Once you have found your way onto a production set, you will begin to see how the work flows through the day. Just like any other job, there are rules, some subtle, some not so subtle, and you will have to find a way to fit into this creative business culture. Here are some common situations found either on location or in a studio and how you should act in them.

Cell Phones and Text Devices

In recent years these devices have become invaluable to all production personnel. From the very basic ability to text a P.A. to assign a task, to "push to talk" technology allowing two-way radio and phone use, one can easily imagine how these kinds of electronics are essential. However, their ubiquity can create issues on a location or set. If you have a text messaging device, it seems an efficient and quiet way to stay in touch. The etiquette there is to avoid becoming so involved with emails and messages that you lose touch with the activity on set.

Just as in a theater or meeting, when on a set or location you *must* use your device's silent function or turn it off. No one on the set is exempt from this rule. It can be quite embarrassing when a ring tone slices into the dialogue of a good take and everyone turns to locate the source of that sound and lays eyes on you. In truth, often it's an agency visitor or even the producer who is guilty of this, but remember, they sign your paycheck!

How to Use Two-Way Radios

On sets or locations, members of the crew are issued two-way radios/ walkie-talkies, which are expensive multi-channel devices. Once provided to you, your name is assigned to the device's number and you become responsible for it. It's also your job to keep track of all of them.

The two-way radios common on sets and locations today have different ranges and accessories; some allow throat microphones and earpieces, others do not. They have channels or frequencies that allow different departments to communicate with one another, while leaving other channels open for general production use.

Typically, production is on channel 1. This is the primary channel for on set cues and directions. Any P.A.s assigned to the set will repeat these cues out loud, such as the most important one, "We're rolling." The A.D.s will speak to P.A.s on this channel, or call them and then switch to another channel to speak off the main channel. Channel 2 is open and available for semi-private conversations. But treat all channels as public, not private. If you don't, you'll soon find out why.

Grip and Electric either share channel 3 or assign their own separate channels.

The nature of two-way communication requires short bursts of conversation or instruction. Its use is *not* like that of a telephone device. So when using the two-way, there are standard modes of speech used on sets and locations.

The term "over" is no longer used on sets. If you use it, you'll be recognized as being inexperienced.

For example:

Locating a person: "What's your twenty?" (What is your location?)

Indicating that you understand or hear the call: "Copy that."

Indicating you are waiting for response: "Come back." The term "over" is no longer used on sets—if you use it, you will be recognized as being inexperienced.

Indicating a need to use a restroom: "I'm ten one hundred."

In order to be certain that you are understood, it is important to press the "key" or "talk" button and hold it until your message is complete, then release the key. When speaking into a two-way, one must keep the unit a few inches from the mouth. If you don't, you might sound like the familiar drive-thru speaker guy.

To contact someone, say your name and whom you are calling, i.e.: "Jim Video to Sean, do you copy?" Again, one does *not* say "over." An alternate might be: "Jim Video to Sean, come back." Call *just once, maybe twice,* but not repeatedly. If the person you are trying to reach doesn't answer, either try to relay from another person with "eyes on" the subject or, if possible, search on foot.

Finally, just as cell phones and pagers need to be silenced, your two-way needs to be silenced or turned way down anywhere near the set where there are many other two-way units (unless of course you have an earpiece). Nothing disrupts work like the squeal of a two-way radio.

TALKING

On a set or location with or without "sync," or sound recording, talking can be disruptive. Before a sound take, you will often hear an A.D. say, "Very quiet please, roll sound, camera, and action." This is a definite cue to stop all talking. Your job may be to help lock down the set and keep it quiet. You and all other P.A.s will repeat, "Rolling, quiet please." When an A.D calls it, you'll need to check for open doors, talkers, and bogeys—stray or unplanned civilians or vehicles in the shot.

Whenever there are crews working in different crafts or areas, idle conversation or work-related talk tends to build to a point where "focus" (of thought) near the camera can be disruptive. So anywhere you are, by the food table or at your station, be aware of this and keep conversation quiet and to a minimum.

APPROACHING TALENT

Approaching talent (actors) is a tricky issue. It depends largely on the stature of the individual and that person's entourage. As a P.A., you might pick up talent at the airport or hotel. In all cases, you simply act professionally and personably and get your job done.

On a set, the best rule is to observe, listen, and generally keep a distance. This also applies to obtaining autographs.

DRESS FOR THE SET

If you're from Michigan you already know—wear layers (for indoor jobs or out!) But in general, you have to be ready for anything on a job, so bring an extra shirt, pair of pants, socks, and shoes. Chances are, you will know what you need, but feel free to ask questions. One thing is for sure, a change of shoes and socks after ten hours on the job *will* refresh you. Black clothing or "show blacks" are often required attire, especially for live shows and events.

A change of shoes and socks after ten hours on the job *will* refresh you.

WEATHER BAG

A weather bag is a good item to have. It is filled with important and necessary items as listed later in this manual. I carry a weather duffle bag. I keep extra clothing and supplies in it for my piece of mind and comfort. As a P.A., a knapsack might be a better choice. Some production personnel can drive near enough to a location so they can keep a duffle bag close. But a P.A. is highly mobile. You need to be able to jump onto a vehicle to get to a new location in a flash with your gear.

As a P.A., a knapsack is a good choice for your weather bag.

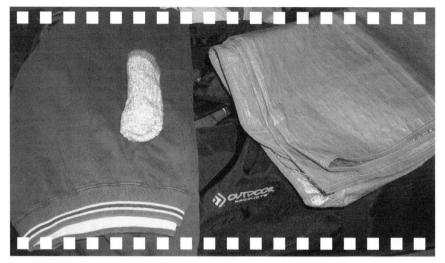

Contents of a weather bag.

What Might Be Found in the Well-Prepared Production Person's Weather Bag
(Items change with the season)

Winter

warm hat, an extra layer (t-shirt, hoodie, sweatshirt, wind-breaker)

light/heavy socks, boots (waterproof), warm gloves

Weather—long days

backup athletic shoes, work gloves

rain gear, shorts or zip-off pants

Protective Items

sun screen, insect repellent, flashlight and extra batteries, weather radio

matches/torch, tarp or fire blanket, lightweight rope

Just Because/Extra Items

playing cards, Frisbee/glove and ball, energy bar, bottled water

Working with talent, using two-way radios, and having the right tools are all important skill sets for any crew member. Let's take a closer look at what is expected on the set.

Chapter 3
Housekeeping and Other Responsibilities
On Set or Location

Dual cameras rigged on a western-style and J.L. Fisher dolly.

Trash Patrol

On a set or location, all departments are at work but not necessarily at the same time or at the same place. In all cases, there will be refuse from construction, from extras waiting in holding areas, and from the craft services table. A set P.A. should be self-motivated to remove excess trash and refuse from working areas. Remember, a P.A. never sits down. Always have a mission in mind to help keep the production safe, clean, and comfortable.

When returning from a mission on the road or anywhere else, make a habit to patrol the stage or location set and watch for empty cans and bottles to recycle and for refuse on the ground, on tables, or near equipment cases. The craft services department will set up recycling boxes or bags near their stations when possible and take them to a facility at the end of the job. As a P.A., you can help by being observant and pitching in when the need arises.

It's also important to check trash containers and refresh them (and sweep around in studio/stage areas) as much as possible. A good example of this is during a corporate or commercial project. Often, a location is used that typically will not accommodate twenty-five or thirty people on a crew. The host location's bathrooms will need extra attention for trash and supplies throughout the day.

When placing trash receptacles, don't forget props, sound, and video as well as script. Trash bins will be needed within a reasonable distance of these work areas.

DRY ROLLING FOR PAINTED FLOORS

On a stage where the floor is either white or black, a P.A. can assist by making sure towels are firmly taped to the deck/floor for shoe bottom cleaning and that trash bins are positioned around the shooting area—out of the way, yet close. Often on this type of painted stage, the production department will have supplied "footies" or "booties," slip-on cotton shoe covers, for the crew. If these items are not available, people should remove their shoes, but you should be ready to "dry roll" the painted areas if footprints are visible. You will also have to dry roll once the various departments have finished their touch-ups.

CRAFTY

Earlier we pointed out that "Crafty" is really the heart of any show, providing comfort in many ways. Quite often, craft services or "client services" as they are referred to on commercial sets, is an entry point for a P.A. You may be hired as a P.A. doing crafts or specifically Craft Services. The difference is how important a budget item this duty is on the project.

In Michigan, Craft Services, at least on feature films, is now a union position and part of the stagehands local. This means that they have a little bit more support behind them for pay rates, work hours, as well as pension and health opportunities. Regardless of this, the position tends to pay about the same as a P.A. rate.

Craft Services can be a big housekeeping issue on sets. On small jobs, responsibilities are to maintain one table. But on a large job, many rolling carts may be required. In either situation, you must be organized and know how to budget for food and beverages for the duration of the project. If the job requires many food locations, be sure to request an assistant. Budgets sometimes do not allow such help, but you should inform the production department that you will need time to set out multiple stations.

Production projects will work in all seasons, so you need to be prepared to set up in a state park or in the parking lot of a major corporation. Since food for the crew tends to be set out on tables near a motor home or under a pop up tent, it is often left out in the hot sun. In such situations it can become a hazard, even on a slow job, if someone were to get sick. Everyone needs to use common sense and put things like dairy products and condiments away—not just Craft Services, but all crew and certainly all P.A.s.

The takeaway from this is if you are hired to work in Craft Services and even if you are not in that department, it can be a bigger undertaking than it seems and the best idea is to keep a watchful eye for food safety.

P.A.'s BIG RESPONSIBILITES
Two-Way Radio Assignments and Tracking

You will be responsible for making a list of radio distribution. Depending on the size of the job, this list may be kept in the A.D. office or the production office. You'll need to make sure names are also written on white tape and adhered to each radio. Always keep an eye out for radios that may have been dropped or misplaced.

Who will need a fresh battery first? The A.D., so be ready!

P.A. on two-way-radio duty.

TRACKING BATTERIES

The first hurdle to jump, when you are responsible for the two-way radios, is to find a home for the cases and charging stations. On a stage, it may be placed on a table near the production staff; on a location, it may be placed in a motor home or the A.D.'s office—anywhere near a power source. Just as with the radios, your function here is to note at various points in the production schedule how many batteries are out and to keep an eye out for lost or misplaced items. *Every* P.A. should have at least one extra two-way battery with them *at all times* on bigger jobs. Who will need a fresh battery first? The A.D., so be ready!

TRACKING HEADSETS

The last piece of the radio puzzle is headsets. Some departments need them for the run of the show. They will fail, as will batteries, and radios will need to be replaced. Keep the headsets handy and near the cases for radios and chargers.

DISTRIBUTION OF SIDES AND CALL SHEETS

Sides are small versions of the script pages to be shot on a particular day. A film measures the day's work in terms of page length accomplished, such as an eighth of a page or two and one eighth pages. A P.A. will be assigned to take the required script pages to the copier to reduce, collate, and put them together with a well-placed staple. This often involves some cutting and fitting. These "sides" are then distributed to the crew each day. Depending on crew size, you might need to make enough for fifty to one hundred people.

The same is true for call sheets. Call sheets contain a listing by department of who in the crew is working and at what time. Additionally, call sheets indicate weather forecasts; if the work is interior or exterior; a snapshot of equipment, props, or sets needed; and more. These information sheets go out several times in a day. On a feature, there will be a preliminary call sheet and then at wrap a final call sheet will be given to P.A.s for distribution. The call sheet will also be emailed to crew on many projects. See the appendix for examples of these forms.

ONE LINERS AND DAY OF DAYS

One liners and Day of Days are also distributed to the crew throughout the production schedule. The one liner is a summary of the current shooting schedule leaving off cast or crew information. The Day of Days is a production sheet that holds more detail than a one liner. It indicates when a crane or camera will be needed and states a page count to be completed.

See the appendix for examples of these forms as well.

FILM OR VIDEO DROP-OFF

This job is often negotiated between the P.A.s. Can you imagine if the P.A., the lowest-paid crew member, didn't drop off the day's work at the lab, lost it, or stole it? It happens.

During any project, whether shooting on film or video, someone must take the finished film or tape to a lab, production office, or editing facility. In some cases, film or video will need to be shipped. You will work with someone more experienced, a camera assistant, producer, or another P.A., to make sure it is prepared correctly. Getting the content of the day's work to its destination is a simple job, but things do happen.

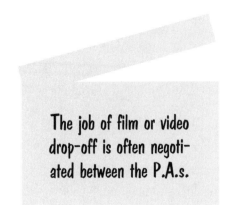

The job of film or video drop-off is often negotiated between the P.A.s.

In New York, a P.A. was to take a cab to the lab. But he had another stop, and forgot the reels in the cab and lost thousands of dollars of work. In Detroit, a P.A. left the film in his trunk overnight, completely forgetting to take it to the lab. I know the Detroit P.A. no longer works in this business. Make it your business to help decide who goes and get it to where it needs to be.

A base camp.

COMPANY MOVES AND CARAVANING

On any project, the crew might need to move to a new location or from a location to a stage. That's called a "company move."

On any move, a P.A. needs to be available to assist. So many things can happen on a company move—especially if there is inclement weather, a fast move, or a long trip—that it is imperative to coordinate with production or other P.A.s to be efficient. The main thing is to get in there and find someone who looks like they might need help. The production algebra here needs to be strong to keep safe, on track, and on time.

> During moves, the main thing is to get in there and find someone who looks like they might need help.

Use your time to facilitate cleanup and exit from the current location *and* make sure all crew and clients make it to the next location.

RENTAL AND PICKUPS

A huge responsibility left with a P.A. is rental pickup and return. It requires some thought and a whole list of do's and don'ts. In conversations with camera assistants and rental facility owners, we've compiled the following list. It deals mostly with camera rentals, but can apply to lighting, sound, or any production supplies.

A PRODUCTION ASSISTANT'S GUIDE TO THE RENTAL HOUSE

- Know the hours of operation for the vendor you are visiting.

- Always ask the Prep Tech or Camera Assistant if the camera magazines are loaded. If so, they need to be stored upright. Do not be afraid to ask, if you are unsure which side is up.

- If you are transporting film, it should be treated with the utmost care and kept in a cool and secure location (ideally in the front cab of the truck). A can of film will need to be replaced if it is dented.

- Always ask if the batteries are charged or if you need to charge them. If you are not sure how to charge batteries, ask.

- Don't leave fluid heads for tripods in a truck overnight in cold weather.

- You are responsible for making sure the batteries are stored properly. They should not be left overnight in cold temperatures or they will lose their charge.

- *Do not leave equipment unattended at any time*, especially when loading and unloading the truck.

- When the vehicle is unattended, all doors should be locked. Check doors before driving off—a loader or second camera assistant may be in the back loading or unloading film.

- Let the A.C. or Prep Tech know *immediately* if you drop a case. If damaged equipment is allowed to make its way to the set, the entire shoot may be delayed until it is replaced. Most Coordinators and Prep Techs will not be angry if you admit to a mistake, but all will be furious if they discover you tried to cover one up.

- Do not open any camera cases out of curiosity. Much of the equipment is extremely fragile and expensive. You should *never* open a case unless you are charging a battery or are instructed to do so by the A.C.

- Gear should be returned by the designated time of the day it is due or the production company will be charged for an extra rental day. If you are delayed, let the Coordinator know as soon as possible so he or she can arrange a deadline extension.

- When returning equipment, do not leave the camera house until the Prep Tech confirms that all cases have been accounted for.

- Keep your cell phone on at all times while you are on duty.

Remember: This is the communications business. Communicate. As a general rule, if you are not sure, ask.

All this knowledge will come in handy on the set. Keep these things in mind as we go through a day on the set in the next chapter.

CHAPTER 4
A DAY IN THE LIFE ON THE SET

Shoot location

Having outlined your responsibilities on a set, let's lay out what a typical day might be like. Report to work at your call time, or even better, at least fifteen minutes early. Be sure to double-check that call time. *Being late is a bad thing.* If you are new, see the production coordinator or an A.D. That might not be an easy thing to do on some sets. If you cannot find the A.D.'s trailer on a feature, or the person who hired you, find someone with a two-way radio and have that person ask the question. If this is the first day of production, things will tend to be a little slow and maybe a little chaotic, but it will be a controlled chaos. Getting that first shot always seems to take the longest time.

In most situations, production staff will note on the call sheet that crew has arrived, as well as when the camera first rolls, and then when each are wrapped. You may even assist in that effort. Your arrival ahead of time provides a harried coordinator, APOC, or A.D. some piece of mind, especially if you are new and an unknown equation.

The equation here is:
Lateness = bad. Early arrival = more work for you.

If you are early enough, have a look around the set and become familiar with it. This is also a time when you can get acquainted with the crew around the craft services/snack table. Note that typically there will be a call time for breakfast, as well as a general call on big jobs. P.A.s are responsible for handing out a production schedule, or the call sheet and sides—digest it

A P.A. always looks for the need to page a cable.

with your breakfast and find out how the day is expected to unfold...at least on paper.

At the appointed call time, an A.D. will call everyone to work. In some cases, an A.D. will go through a talk about safety. Listen carefully. Everyone is expected to be present for this information, especially if there are to be stunts or special effects. If the A.D. or production department has not already directed you to do a job, listen and observe. Be available to any department that asks for help.

THINGS YOU WILL OBSERVE DURING THE DAY

The A, or primary, camera crew will be blocking the first scene and/or shot. Blocking is the positioning of talent and set pieces. The art, set, and props departments will be working on final touches for this scene while talent rehearses lines and gets microphones placed on their wardrobe. Dolly track will be laid down and leveled, and then the camera will rehearse its movement.

If all is ready, the 1st A.D. will call for action and several takes will be captured. In order to ensure that all the actors are seen in relation to one another, many different angles are shot. This is called "coverage." You will see a wide shot, then a medium shot, a close-up, an over-the-shoulder shot,

A director's workspace.

and a reverse shot for each actor present. Quite like a factory, all departments will work through the day to capture the required script pages from all of these angles.

Lunch is usually called six hours after the general crew call based on prevailing union contracts. On corporate and commercial jobs, P.A.s will be needed to help set up tables and chairs or assist the caterer in getting to the meal area. Do not invite guests or visitors for lunch without the permission of the production department, either the Producer, Coordinator, or A.D.

Union crew must go through the line first. If there are extras or other talent on set, you need to make sure they understand this. Sometimes you will find that talent has a box lunch, which means they can be routed to a different line.

This would also be a great time to help "Crafty" by moving coolers to the lunch area.

The lunch break is generally one half hour (occasionally it can be one hour) and begins when the last union member receives their food.

Lunch officially begins when the last union member receives their food.

After lunch, it's back to work. There are no other scheduled breaks during the day. Individual crew can usually find a few minutes when time allows to grab a pick-me-up. Craft Services is set up close to the set to facilitate this.

The day will normally run ten to twelve hours. Be aware that often locations are far from home which could add as much as one hour each way to your day.

At the end of each shoot day, P.A.s will be assigned to help clean up, return equipment or props, and make the film drop. In some cases, on longer jobs in one location, you'll hear the term "walk away." "Walk away" means everyone will wrap cables back for safety, secure the set and equipment, and go home instead of loading or moving.

Repeating what has been covered earlier, if you are given the responsibility of making the film drop, be aware that the day's work and a lot of money is in your hands. Be safe; get the film there safely and to the right place.

At some point near the end of the day/job, you will be asked to fill out forms that allow you to be paid as well as forms required by either the government and/or the client. Be certain to have a conversation with your producer, coordinator, or A.D. *prior* to the job about your pay rate, if you'll receive overtime, and when you can expect to be paid.

Be certain to have a conversation with your producer, coordinator, or A.D. prior to the job about your pay rate, if you'll receive overtime, and when you can expect to be paid.

TYPICAL FORMS

- The I-9 is an immigration form, which proves citizenship. Be sure to have your driver's license and Social Security information available.

- The payroll and W-2 contain workday information such as hours worked. This is usually several carbonless pages, which include the W-2 tax withholding information form.

- A non-disclosure agreement signed by you ensures that you understand that items or images you have seen while working on the project are private and not to be discussed outside of the set.

The appendix contains examples of these forms.

Some projects use a payroll service such as "Spotlight" or "Cast and Crew." If so, that will be how you record your hours for payment. Their forms usually have a vendor copy that you can keep for your records. On multiple-day jobs, make sure that you keep an

On multiple-day jobs, make sure that you keep an accurate record of your billable hours, mileage, and any billable equipment.

accurate record of your billable hours, mileage, and any billable equipment. Our experience is that the days roll into one another, and at the end of the week you may become confused about in-times, lunch times, and out-times. On those projects where a payroll firm is not used, have your invoice ready to fill out. You can use any number of templates for an invoice found online. Either Excel or Word documents are acceptable.

It's one thing to work on the set and follow directions. But, as you have read, in order to organize your schedule you need to keep track of a lot of details. One of those details is exactly what the pay rates are for a P.A. We will go over that in the next chapter and discuss a bit more about the intricacies of scheduling freelance work. Finally, it's a good idea to review the glossary, forms, and other information in the appendix.

CHAPTER 5
PAY RATES AND SCHEDULING

Pay rates are determined prior to getting the job. Many positions on a motion picture are covered by a union, but at present P.A.s are not part of one. P.A.s earn between $125 and $250 a day. But as a freelancer, you are responsible for paying your own taxes on a quarterly basis, plus pension and health insurance. Speak with your accountant or tax professional about how to deal with this important issue.

Again, make sure to check with the Production Department prior to the job to determine if you are being paid on a flat day rate or overtime after ten hours.

Because the pay is better than in many day jobs, production jobs are called the golden cage—once you taste this pay, you don't want to do anything else.

Traditionally, pay for commercial work is higher than for feature films because commercials are short-time jobs. A P.A. might earn $250 per day plus overtime after ten hours on a commercial. But on a feature film, they will earn $125 per day plus overtime after twelve or even fourteen hours. Also, as mentioned earlier, films use a payroll service so you can choose your taxable rate and not have to worry about paying quarter taxes. Do speak with a tax professional when you start to earn a living in the freelance world.

SCHEDULING

When you are in a position to be hired for a project, there are some important concerns to know. When you get a call for work, you will be asked for your availability for a given period of time, whether it is a day or a month. You must be organized enough to say with confidence that you are or are not available.

Your availability is gauged by three terms, a "hold," a "pencil," or a "book." It can also be more nuanced by the concepts of a first, second, and third call or hold.

Nine times out of ten, you can simply accept the job and write the date in your planner. That said, here is the conundrum that happens often enough to mention: once you accept a job, there will be another one offered either on the same day or during the same week. Sometimes when you accept a job for a day, a three-day job will be offered overlapping your one day. What do you do?

Simply stated, you must be responsible to the first person that calls. This is your "first hold."

After a relationship has been established and if there is enough time before the job, you might be able to ask your producer if you can back out of a hold to accept a longer commitment or replace yourself with another trusted P.A. Don't do this often—it is a bridge burner. Most importantly, if your replace yourself, make sure the person you recommend will do a good job. This person now represents you and your reputations are tied.

This can become complicated. You might find yourself with several phone calls for holds. If you have not been booked, that is, confirmed on a project, you order the holds by first, second, or maybe third. The first one to book you gets your services. The best idea here is to communicate with other P.A.s on their experiences. Be cautious and use a good scheduling resource—calendar or electronic planner.

Be careful to ask if you are shooting at night, as you could get caught working from 8PM to 6AM one day then, 8AM to 6PM the next day.

Be careful to ask if you are shooting at night, as you could get caught working from 8PM to 6AM one day then, 8AM to 6PM the next day.

Double booking should be avoided. If you accept two jobs on the same day, that is called double booking. If you are not organized, you can fall into this situation. You can offend both producers and lose future work. In all of these cases, know your schedule.

Occasionally, you will find that a day runs short, and if you know this in advance you might be able to accept a job which starts later the same day. This is considered "double dipping." It can be done—but if that first project runs long, your risk is the same as double booking. It is best to avoid this because, as a P.A., you have little control of your schedule.

Mileage Reports

Another term for a P.A. is a "runner." So it can be assumed that some of your time will be spent driving. You will be sent on missions to get special coffee for the producer, pick up or drop off equipment, or drive people to the airport or to a hotel. You will be reimbursed for your mileage, so you must keep an accurate record of it. A mileage form is included in the appendix for your review. Mileage rates are set by the IRS, and at time of publication they stand at fifty-five cents per mile.

In your travels you will be making purchases and, as we have mentioned earlier in this manual, you will need to keep track of receipts and general spending. A sample petty cash form is also included in the appendix. Your receipts must be affixed to 8 1/2 x 11 paper and identified clearly in addition to the use of the petty cash form. If you don't have a receipt for an item, you will have to have some proof of the item's purchase. Occasionally, you may be able to "buy" a receipt from another P.A. This kind of transaction, as well as many others we have discussed, will become clearer when you work with other P.A.s with more experience. The relationships you form will be long lasting and the foundations upon which you can build your career.

CONCLUSION
MARTINI SHOT

Throughout this training manual, we have discussed the wide variety of tasks and positions you will find in production jobs. We have provided a glimpse at pay rates, the equipment you might use, and a bit of philosophy in a code of conduct. Our goal in this has been to help you as a new P.A. fit into the equation that is the production community worldwide.

Whether you find yourself working on an electronic field production crew of four in Chicago or a feature film crew of 154 in Detroit, your job as a P.A. will be to support them, whatever it takes.

Remember always that making a motion picture, be it a corporate, commercial, or feature film, is a large undertaking. The business of such filmmaking is very expensive and creates an expectation to get the job done in a fast and efficient manner. The people at the top have earned their places by doing this and they expect you to do the same.

While your basic job description sounds simple—basic math, knowledge of geographic areas, readiness to paint, refresh trash, and direct traffic—it has many challenges. The algebra needed to be effective and grow in this industry includes in large part self-motivation and organizational skills. You will work with different personalities and egos. It will take patience and require you to listen well. Funny thing, though—when asked, A.D.s always say your best tools are your mind, a pencil, and paper.

In summary, Job = (Passion x Organizational skills) +
(Common Sense x Forethought x Follow-through)

A passion for the craft is nice, but common sense, forethought, and follow-through will be the winning formula to earn you your next job.

APPENDIX

Tips for Getting a Job

Standard Crew List

Glossary of Common Film Production Terms and Set Terminology

A.D. Lingo on Set

AICP Filmmakers Code

Perspective on P.A.s by Production Manager Jason Wolk from New York

Basic List of Industry Organizations

Forms

Tips for Getting a Job—Common Sense and More

- A strong, literate cover letter is very important. This means proper spelling and grammar throughout. You need to sell yourself and whatever skills you have in this people-oriented business that involves long hours and many demands. Clearly lay out your goals and what you can do to support a production.

- Start your job search in areas where you have a realistic chance. Send resumes to companies that produce smaller projects like corporate or industrial videos, even public access television. People who start in these areas often cross over to broadcast television and features, but to aim for features and television while attempting to gain experience is not reasonable and, in all likelihood, will be met with rejection.

- Work as an extra on a film or commercial. Opportunities may occur where you can meet with crew members and perhaps win an entry-level job.

- Take any entry-level job, no matter how distant from your goal, and do the best job you can and meet everyone. In the production industry, more than any other business, who you know may be the fastest route to your destination.

- Jobs are based on recommendations ("recommends") by people who have hired you in the past. This should be good motivation to develop a strong, lasting relationship with people in all departments. Conversely, it is said by experienced crew members that you must be nice to P.A.s because down the road they may hire you.

- Subscribe to publications like *American Cinematographer*, *Student Filmmaker Magazine*, and *Variety*, or online publications like *Shoot* (www.shootonline.com) and *Below the Line* (www.btlnews.com). These will keep you up to date and informed on what is happening in the film and video industry. List yourself in guides like your state's Film Office Resource Guide and on Mandy.com. If your contact info changes, update it everywhere! It's inexpensive and the first job you get more than pays for the listing fee.

- Immerse yourself in the industry. Go to seminars and workshops and get involved in film-related organizations such as the Michigan Production Alliance and the Chicago Film Industry Meetup Group. Networking is key. Get to know as many people in the industry as you can and ask them to help you.

- If you can afford to, volunteer your services on a commercial or film/television production. It will give you experience and put you around the people you need to know. Once you gain this experience, be cautious of giving services away. But when starting out, giving services away can make a difference. If you are enrolled in a community college or university, check with your school to see if you can get credit for volunteering. In all cases, be polite, professional, and remember that you need them, not vice versa. Concentrate on ways you can be an asset to the project.

- The nature of our industry and related jobs is that they are short-term and project-oriented and therefore, as a rule, we are all independent contractors or freelancers, not employees—though that is changing in subtle ways.

- It's not only whom you know and what you know, but also what you have done and what you have done lately. In other words, you are always positioning yourself for the next job while maintaining your current job. If you are smart and maintain a positive attitude, you won't burn your bridges behind you, making it impossible to return. Our experience has told us that ignorance of the nature of the business and how hiring really works can make your efforts flat and unprofitable.

- Your best opportunity to build your credit list is to work on smaller independent shoots. You can try public access TV or theater as well. Track these shoots down and volunteer! Once your resume begins to show the depth of your experience, you can start to aim for bigger crews on larger shoots. Always tell a prospective client what you have done lately.

- If you send a resume to a company, have a contact name and follow it up with a phone call within a week, then try to visit the person you sent it to. Then stay in touch by phone.

- Phone a list of potential clients every month. Tell them what you have been working on and that you are available.

- Get and use a functional organizer. You'll need to be able to view at a glance when you are available for jobs.

- Learn how to use production software and always seek out ways to improve your skills.

These are basic tips that can be found in many job search publications. Adapt them to your own personal style and present yourself as a professional with a clear voice and good attitude.

STANDARD CREW LIST

Development

Executive Producer: Typically this is the person in charge of all finances and producers on a film production.

Producer: The organizer and overall coordinator of a project.

Line Producer: Responsible for the financial and business aspects of the project on a set.

Production Department

Director: The creative person in charge.

Assistant Director (A.D.): Runs the set logistically and maintains the shooting schedule.

2nd Assistant Director: Often issues the project's call sheets. Other responsibilities include coordinating with crew.

3rd Assistant Director: Utility position and learning the job. Helps out coordinating actors and background as the 2nd A.D. might do.

Production Manager or Unit Production Manager: Oversees day-to-day financial requirements and often hires and manages crew.

Coordinator: Operates under the Line Producer, Producer or Production Manager. The coordinator is the frontline organizer on set.

Location Manager and Location Scout: Both positions assist the Creative team in finding/securing suitable production locations. Also are responsible for coordinating between business/home/property owners and production departments.

All members of the Production Department are members in the Directors Guild of America (DGA).

CAMERA DEPARTMENT

Director of Photography (D.P.): Handles overall photographic look of the project in concert with the Creative team. Coordinates with technical crew, particularly camera department, grip, and electric.

Camera operator: Physically operates the camera, frames shots, works closely with the D.P., grip, and electric departments on maintaining the established look of the project.

1st Camera Assistant (A.C.): One primary job is "focus puller" and often determines F and T stops and records focal lengths, distances, and ratios based upon lenses used. Responsible for all camera equipment and reports. Loads magazines, checks mechanisms for debris, and maintains film inventory.

2nd Assistant: Works with 1st Assistant on maintaining camera equipment. Loads magazines, assists with reports, inventories, and slating duties.

All members of the Camera Department are members of the International Alliance of Theatrical and Stage Employees (IATSE).

TECHNICAL CREW

Sound Department

Production Sound Mixer: Records sound for each scene, mixes levels for each take. Maintains best quality of sound on location or in the studio. Determines microphone placement on actors and on the set.

Boom Operator: Handles the sound boom. Often assists mixer in microphone placement and best location for the boom.

Video Assist Technician: Records rehearsals and each take for evaluation by the creative team.

All members of the Sound Department are members of the International Alliance of Theatrical and Stage Employees (IATSE). The sound mixer can also be a member of the Cinema Audio Society (CAS).

Grip/Electric Department

Gaffer: Head of Lighting Department. Works directly with Director and D.P. Determines lighting and electrical needs for the project. The term "gaffer's tape" derives from this. Gaffer's tape looks very similar to duct tape but is different, and since it's used in film production, costs much, much more, of course. Like duct tape, its uses are limitless.

Key Grip: Determines lighting hardware needs and supervises grips who are responsible for setting up and striking stands, instruments, platforms, cranes and/or scaffolding that allow cameras, lights, or other equipment to be positioned for each shot.

Best Boy: Flexible term. Works with the grips often from the grip truck as its coordinator. In some cases, the Best Boy operates and maintains a generator on a set. Essentially, this position is the gaffer's assistant.

Dolly Grip: Designated grip responsible for all aspects related to the dolly on a set. Moves the dolly as instructed, adjusts wheels, elevating arm, levels track, and helps 1st A.C. secure a camera to the dolly.

Script Supervisor: Works closely with the Director taking notes and tracking details involved in each shot. Maintains a log of this information and is responsible for maintaining continuity throughout the project.

Props (property master): Researches, buys, or rents all items needed for project. Often must dress the set and maintain continuity of this aspect of the project.

Vanities

Makeup/Hair: Styles hair/applies makeup for performers as necessary. Often two positions depending upon size of project.

Wardrobe: Often responsible for searching for appropriate clothing or costumes for a project. Responsible for costume continuity and maintenance. Helps actors or background dress.

All members of the Grip/Electric, Vanities, and Wardrobe Departments are members of the International Alliance of Theatrical and Stage Employees (IATSE).

Car Prep: Responsible for all aspects of any picture vehicles on a project. Removes or applies accessories to the vehicle and keeps it clean.

Production Assistant: Often a runner or a "gopher" (go for) on a set, and the glue holding together any production. Responsible to any department and assigned by a coordinator or producer to accomplish tasks. Tasked to find items for the project such as office supplies. The P.A. must pick up film and later drop it off for processing. This position can move into a specific department to assist, i.e. Camera P.A. It's where you pay your dues before moving up the production ladder.

Craft Services/Client Services: This position is responsible for providing light meals and snacks to the crew and production team. Often runs to get related supplies and items for crew members that cannot leave the set.

Glossary of Common Film Production Terms and Set Terminology

Aspect ratio: The ratio of width to height of a film frame or screen. In the early days, the most common aspect ratio, often called "Academy Aperture," was 1.33:1, read as "one thirty-three to one," (a television screen has this aspect ratio but is usually referred to as a 4:3 aspect ratio). Standard widescreen aspect ratio is 1.85:1; Cinemascope and other anamorphic systems have a 2.35:1 AR, while 70mm formats have an AR of 2.2:1.

Cross-cutting: Cutting between two (or more) actions that are related to each other, and occurring simultaneously, but in different locations. This technique is very effective in building tension or suspense, and was perfected by early film pioneer and genius D. W. Griffith.

Cut: A instantaneous transition from one shot to the next. So-called because the film was actually cut and spliced to the next piece. Its basic functions are to serve as a continuity device, to allow for camera angle changes, or to move from one location to another. It's also what a director shouts during filming to end the action and stop a shot or "take."

Digital loader: An emerging position. Requires strong computer skills. A digital loader or "data wrangler" is responsible for managing visual data on HD productions.

Dissolve: A transition from one shot to the next by overlapping the two. In essence, one shot fades out while the other fades in on top of it. Its common uses are to indicate the passage of time, to give a softer touch to shot changes, to slow down the pace of a sequence, or to indicate a flashback or flash-forward. It provides a different emotional tone to the transition than does the cut.

Dolly: As a noun, it is a device on wheels that is moved along a set of tracks to give the camera mobility and smoothness. There are several different types and sizes, but all are designed to do the same thing—provide a moving platform for the camera. As a verb, it means to physically move the camera towards or away from the action (see "tracking shot"). Cameras "track" left or right, and "dolly" in (toward the action) or out (away from the action).

Down converter: A devise used on HD or high definition video shoots to allow or convert the HD signal to an NTSC or composite signal for use with non-HD monitors and equipment.

Establishing shot: Usually the first shot of a scene which establishes the spatial relationships and physical layout of the frame. Most commonly, this is a wide shot so that most, if not all, of the space can be seen.

Fade: There are two types of fades: The fade-in and the fade-out. Fade-in means to gradually bring up a shot from a (usually) black screen to full intensity. A fade-out is the opposite—to go from a full intensity image to black (or, occasionally, other colors).

Montage: This may be the most overused and misunderstood term in film. "Montage" does not necessarily mean "fast-cutting," although it may apply to such a technique. But it has other definitions, and montages come in many forms. In general, montages work by the association or contrasting of images to create concepts and ideas that are not specifically contained in the images themselves.

Pan: A pan is the left-to-right (or right-to-left) movement of the camera from a fixed position such as a tripod. In a pan, the camera doesn't physically move from its location, but merely pivots left or right on a vertical axis, giving a horizontal movement across the frame.

POV: A "point-of-view" shot. A shot that gives the viewer the subjective view of the character.

Permalancer: A newly coined term that indicates a freelance person who works more or less full time for one company without benefits.

Per diem: A daily allowance for expenses. This is specified in union contracts and common for crew members to receive, especially when on location projects.

Racking/pulling focus: This refers to a change in the focus characteristics of the image during the shot. Either the background or foreground will be in clear focus with the other blurred. By racking or pulling focus, these fields are reversed. It's a device that allows a director to control what a viewer sees and when.

Shot: Also called a "take," it's the image captured on film from the time a camera starts rolling until it stops. It is the basic cinematic unit, which can be as short as a single frame, or as in the case of some experimental structural films, an entire reel of film.

Slate: The clapboard that has the shot and other information on it. It is filmed at the start of each shot so that the information is available to the editor. Originally, the moveable clapsticks were snapped together to give the editor a synchronizing point for the audio and picture image. Modern slates display similar information about the shot, but also provide a time-code display.

SteadiCam: The SteadiCam is a device that mounts the camera on the operator's body. A system of springs and counterbalancing devices provides for remarkable smoothness and mobility, and allows for an "in-the-action" kind of look for the viewer. The development of lightweight cameras allowed for the subsequent development of the SteadiCam in the 1970s.

Tilt: A tilt is the vertical movement of a camera from a fixed position (see "pan"). Cameras "tilt" up or down.

Tracking shot: Here the camera itself does actually move either left or right, usually along a line parallel to the action it's filming. But tracking can also be done in other ways, such as following or leading the action. An "arcing" shot is one where the camera tracks around the action in a circular path.

Work flow: A method for efficiently processing captured images. The introduction of hard drives and capture cards necessitates a smooth model for saving images redundantly and getting the drive or card back into production.

Zoom: A zoom lens is one that allows for a change in focal length during the shot. One can "zoom in," which enlarges the image on the screen, or "zoom out" which reduces the image size. Often thought of as a substitute for a dolly shot, it's quite different, and it gives a very different visual effect.

A.D. Lingo on Set

Abby singer: The second-to-last shot of the day.

Action: Main action begins.

Back to one: All elements return to starting positions.

Background action: Extras, vehicles, or the like begin movement.

Bells or "on bells": When the Sound Mixer makes a bell sound to quiet the area.

Blocking: Setting marks for actors, cameras, props, and settings.

Bogeys: Stray and unplanned civilians or vehicles that may enter a shot.

Check the gate: When the Director is satisfied with a take, the Camera Assistant checks the camera's internal movement for dust or anomalies.

Choker: Extreme close-up or just a close-up.

Clear the eye line: Move away from the sightlines between the camera and talent.

Company move: The crew and talent make a major move to a new location.

Coverage: Different angles or sizes of a particular shot.

Cut: When all action stops.

Final touches: All departments make final adjustments before a shot.

First team: Main talent/stars—not stand-ins.

Hero: The main or real thing—car or prop.

Holding the roll: Wait mode for many reasons (planes, noise, malfunctions).

Honeywagon: A group of trailers with washrooms and dressing rooms.

Hot set: A working set left for another for various reasons.

In the can: Shot or scene is good.

Lock it up: P.A.s secure the perimeter of the set. They watch for bogeys. This phrase will be heard just before the A.D.s call "rolling!"

Main unit: Primary shooting crew.

Martini/fat lady: Last shot of the day or shoot.

Master: Wide shot.

MOS: Motion without sound/no sound. A designation on a slate indicating that a shot is being done "mit out sound" (without sound), which derived from the accent of many early German film directors...or so it is said.

New deal/moving on: After gate is clean on a good take, the company moves to the next scene or coverage angle.

On a roll/series: Camera continues to roll as action repeats.

Pick up: Shooting action from a point other than the beginning.

Picture's up: Ready to shoot.

Roll sound/camera: A.D. calls for cameras and sound to roll.

Room tone: Sound coverage. All is silent for thirty seconds.

Second sticks: Check the take number and place the slate back in for camera or sound.

Speed: When sound, camera, and video record modes are stable and locked in.

Take: One shot.

Video village: Home of monitors and chairs for video assist viewing.

Walk away: Stop what you are doing and leave the area.

Watch your back: Objects are in motion around you.

We're back: Back from lunch or a period of down time.

AICP Filmmakers Code

The "AICP" - Association of Independent Commercial Producers established a code that we as filmmakers can all follow...because we'd like to work in the same place again. We can do this by keeping vendors and homeowners happy.

COMMERCIAL FILMMAKERS' CODE OF PROFESSIONAL RESPONSIBILITY

To the Public: We are pleased to be filming in this location and appreciate your cooperation. If you find this production company is not adhering to this Code, please call _____

at _____.

To our Company: You are guests and should treat this location, as well as the public, with courtesy. This notice has been attached to the filming notification which was distributed to this neighborhood.

1. When filming in a neighborhood or business district, proper notification is to be provided to each merchant or resident who is directly affected by the company (this includes parking, traveling shots, base camps, meal areas, etc.)

2. Production vehicles arriving on location in or near a residential neighborhood shall not enter the area before the time stipulated in the permit. They should park one by one, turning off engines as soon as possible.

Cast and crew shall observe designated parking areas only. Do not park production vehicles in or block driveways without the express permission of the municipal jurisdiction or the driveway owner.

3. Do not trespass onto neighbors' or merchants' property. Remain within the boundaries of the property that has been permitted for filming.

4. Moving or towing of the public's vehicles is prohibited without the express permission of the municipal jurisdiction or the owner of the vehicle.

5. Cast and crew meals shall be confined to the area designated in the location agreement or permit. Use company-supplied receptacles for the disposal of all napkins, plates, and coffee cups that are used in the course of the working day. All catering, craft service, construction, strike, and personal trash must be removed from location.

6. Removing, trimming, and/or cutting of vegetation or trees is prohibited unless approved by the permit authority or the property owner.

7. All signs erected or removed for filming purposes will be removed or replaced upon completion of the use of that location unless otherwise stipulated by the location agreement or permit. Also, remember to remove all signs posted to direct the company to the location.

8. Every member of the cast and crew shall keep noise levels as low as possible.

9. Observe designated smoking areas and always extinguish cigarettes in butt cans.

10. Crew members shall not display signs, posters, or pictures on or in vehicles that do not reflect common sense or good taste (i.e., pin-up posters). Cast and crew will refrain from the use of lewd or improper language.

---

appreciates your cooperation and assistance in upholding the Filmmakers' Code of Professional Responsibility.

This form can be found at www.aicp.com.

Basic List of Industry Organizations

Many positions on film and video shoots are filled with union labor. For anyone who wishes to work in the industry, it's important to know a little bit about the unions and which local represents each craft.

African American TV & Filmmakers – Illinois

The African American TV & Filmmakers (AATF) is a not-for-profit, tax exempt organization that was incorporated in February of 1997, in Chicago, Illinois to bridge a gap in media representation for diversity of African Americans in the television and film industries. AATF provides a building block of cultural diversity in education and support performances in these industries as well as the preservation and cultural awareness.

Director's Guild of America (DGA)
http://www.dga.org

The Director's Guild of America represents more than twelve thousand members working in U.S. cities and abroad. Their creative work is represented in theatrical, industrial, educational, and documentary films and television, as well as videos and commercials.

IATSE 600
http://www.cameraguild.com

With nearly five thousand members—Directors of Photography, Camera Operators, Assistants, Still Photographers, Visual Effects, Animation and Video Specialists—Local 600 may be the largest IATSE local and a major influence in our industry.

THE INTERNATIONAL BROTHERHOOD OF ELECTRICAL WORKERS
http://www.ibew.com

The IBEW represents many employees in the broadcasting industry. With over three hundred collective bargaining agreements, our members are engaged in every aspect of the industry—television and radio stations, network operations, public broadcast stations, recording companies, closed circuit television, and production companies. These members assemble, install, repair, or maintain all materials, equipment, apparatus, and appliances required to transmit data, voice, sound, video, and other emerging technologies. High degrees of skill are required to install, operate, and maintain the complex equipment; and continually changing technology demands personal ingenuity, initiative, and continual skill improvement. Similarly, the recording industry depends upon the special skills of our members in the diverse technical operations required to produce digital audio and video.

MEDIA COMMUNICATIONS ASSOCIATION INTERNATIONAL (MCAI)
http://www.mca-i.org
http://www.detroitmcai.org

The MCAI (formerly ITVA) is an international organization of over nine thousand members worldwide serving the professional needs of visual communicators. Members are in corporate, educational, government, medical, military, and just about every other type of setting where there is a need for professional video communicators. The association provides networking opportunities for its members and also seeks to advance the video profession and promote the growth of quality video and related media. MCAI provides opportunities for professional growth and career advancement as well as an international network for the exchange of ideas and information between individual members. Members can draw on each other's expertise and resources to enhance their careers and professional development.

MICHIGAN FILM OFFICE (MFO)
http://www.michiganfilmoffice.org

The State of Michigan operates the Michigan Film Office (MFO). It is located in Lansing, and tasked to promote commercial and feature film production. They have a website and publish a production resources guide which includes all crafts, union and non-union, video, film, photography, writers, production companies—anyone involved in the creative or administrative aspects of production.

MICHIGAN FILM OFFICE ADVISORY COMMISSION (MFOAC)
http://www.michiganfilmoffice.org

The Michigan Film Office Advisory Commission that had been dormant for many years was reinitiated in 2002 to assist the Michigan Film Office in promoting Michigan as a location, equipment suppliers, and talent. It is a fifteen-person commission appointed by the Governor. This commission is diverse in makeup. Some members work in the industry, some represent unions. Its membership can be found on the MFO website.

MICHIGAN PRODUCTION ALLIANCE (MPA)
http://www.mpami.org

"The Voice of the Production Community." The mission of the Michigan Production Alliance is to offer leadership in the development of incentives and a more stable financial environment for Michigan film and video production companies, freelancers, and support services, and to provide cohesiveness to the community through communications, continuing education, and political awareness.

AMERICAN FEDERATION OF TELEVISION & RADIO ARTISTS (AFTRA)
http://www.aftra.com

AFTRA represents actors and other professional performers and broadcasters in television, radio, sound recordings, non-broadcast/industrial programming, and new technologies such as interactive programming and CD ROMs.

SCREEN ACTORS GUILD (SAG)
http://www.sag.org

The main goal of SAG is to provide competitive wages and safe, excellent working conditions for our members. It's vital to note that SAG *does not* function as some other labor unions in the sense that we *do not* have a hiring hall and *do not* directly provide employment for our members. Our members, like all principal and background performers, must take their own steps towards developing their professional skills, and then getting agents, auditions, and roles. Through a variety of programs and activities and industry outreach, we do everything possible to create an environment in which our members will be hired and look after their welfare once they are hired. The best thing we can do for you at the beginning of your career is to point you towards other sources of information.

THE SOCIETY OF MOTION PICTURE AND
TELEVISION ENGINEERS (SMPTE)
http://www.smpte.org

The Society of Motion Picture and Television Engineers is the leading technical society for the motion imaging industry. Today, SMPTE publishes ANSI-approved Standards, Recommended Practices, and Engineering Guidelines, along with the highly regarded SMPTE Journal and its peer-reviewed technical papers. SMPTE holds conferences and local section meetings to bring people and ideas together, allowing for useful interaction and information exchange.

INTERNATIONAL BROTHERHOOD OF TEAMSTERS (IBT)
http://www.teamster.org

Teamsters drive all vehicles on high-end commercials and feature films. To make life better for Teamster members and their families—and for all working families—the Teamsters organize the unorganized, make workers' voices heard in the corridors of power, negotiate contracts that make the American dream a reality for millions, protect workers' health and safety, and fight to keep jobs in North America. Today's Teamsters are a community of workers, fueled by a contagious spirit that is equal part compassion, commitment, creativity, solidarity, and strength. Collectively, we are dedicated to the ultimate tenet of the trade union movement—the commitment to enhance the lives of our members all across North America...and to win justice for working families.

UAW
http://www.uaw.org

The International Union, United Automobile, Aerospace and Agricultural Implement Workers of America (UAW) is one of the largest and most diverse unions in North America, with members in virtually every sector of the economy. UAW-represented workplaces range from multinational corporations, small manufacturers, and state and local governments to colleges and universities, hospitals, and private non-profit organizations. The UAW has approximately 710,000 active members and over 500,000 retired members in the United States, Canada, and Puerto Rico.

WOMEN IN FILM
http://www.wif.org

Women In Film is a non-profit organization dedicated to helping women achieve their highest potential within the global entertainment, communications, and media industries, and to preserving the legacy of women within those industries.

Founded in 1973, Women In Film and its Women In Film Foundation provide for members an extensive network of contacts, educational programs, scholarships, film finishing funds and grants, access to employment opportunities, mentorships, and numerous practical services in support of this mission.

FORMS

Crew Day of Days

CATEGORY	NAME	TELEPHONE	ALTERNATE #	RATE		M	T	W	TH	F	S	SN	M	T	W	TH	F	S	SN	M	T	W	TH	F	S	SN
DIRECTOR																										
EXEC. PRODUCER																										
PRODUCER																										
ASSIST DIRECTOR																										
2nd A. D.																										
PROD. MANAGER																										
PROD. COORD.																										
DIR. of PHOTO																										
1st ASSIST CAM.																										
2nd ASSIST CAM.																										
SCRIPT																										
GAFFER																										
BEST BOY ELEC.																										
3rd ELECTRIC																										
KEY GRIP																										
BEST BOY GRIP																										
DOLLY GRIP																										
CRANE GRIP																										
GRIP																										
RECORDIST																										
BOOM																										
VIDEO ASSIST																										
STYLIST																										
HAIR / MAKE-UP																										
PROP MASTER																										
PROP ASSIST																										
CRAFT SERVICES																										
PROD. ASSIST																										
PROD. ASSIST																										
PROD. ASSIST																										
PROD. ASSIST																										
PROD. ASSIST																										

ODUCTION CO :
JOB # :
NCY / CLIENT :

"Day of Days" snapshot of actors' work schedule

	35	EXT. TRAIN STATION	Night	1	1/8	
Game 1		The crowd begins to arrive.				
	50	EXT. TRAIN STATION	Night	1	1 2/8	1, 2, 7, 8, 9, 10, 11
Game 1		Tech thanks Cruise for coming out.				8X

Move To Fox Theater

	10	INT. CHRYSLER 300	Night	1	1/8	3
		Vaughn gets stopped by police.				
	11	EXT. SEVEN MILE ROAD	Night	1	2/8	3
		Vaughn receives money from cop.				
	161	EXT. SEVEN MILE RD.	Night	18	1/8	3, 34
		Vaughn gets pulled over again.				
	162	INT. CHRYSLER 300	Night	18	3/8	3, 34
		Officer tells Vaughn they don't like publicity.				

--- END OF DAY 20 -- Sun, Aug 14, 2005 -- 2 3/8 pgs.

Court 1	111	EXT. COURT	Day	7	2/8	1, 8
Montage For 106		Tech and Up continue to win.				
Court 1	115	EXT. COURT	Day	9	1/8	1, 8
Montage For 106		Tech and Up on the hustle again.				
Court 1	116	EXT. COURT	Day	9	1/8	1, 8
Montage For 106		Tech and Up kicking ass.				
Court 1	6	EXT. BASKETBALL COURT	Night	1	4/8	1, 8
		Tech and Up shoot hoops.				
Court 1	20	EXT. BASKETBALL COURT	Night	1	2/8	1, 8
		Tech gets the call.				
Court 1	21A	EXT. BASKETBALL COURT	Night	1	3/8	1, 8
		Cruise says he's coming				
Court 1	160	EXT. COURT	Night	18	3	1, 2
		Cruise trys to apologize to Tech.				

--- END OF DAY 21 -- Mon, Aug 15, 2005 -- 4 5/8 pgs.

Court 1	66	EXT. COURT	Day	2	1 2/8	1, 8
		Tech realizes Up has some moves.				
Court 1	80	EXT. COURT	Dusk	2	1/8	1
		Tech practices some more.				
	27	EXT. STREET	Night	1	3/8	1, 8
		Tech and Up practice their moves in the street.				
	31	EXT. HOUSE	Night	1	5/8	10, 11
		Double A comes by for Stretch.				
	163	EXT. VANESSA'S HOUSE	Night	18	2 5/8	2, 4
		Vanessa tells Cruise he's not the father.				

Move to Store

| | 26 | INT. GROCERY STORE | Night | 1 | 1/8 | 9 |
| | | Big Man bags groceries. | | | | |

--- END OF DAY 22 -- Tue, Aug 16, 2005 -- 5 1/8 pgs.

	173	INT. CAB/ EXT BARBER SHOP	Day	20	6/8	1, 5
		Eboni places bet for Tech.				
	120	EXT. TECH'S HOUSE	Day	12	2/8	1, 2, 4, 5, 7
		Jewelz and Vanessa exchange looks.				
	156	EXT. TECH'S HOUSE	Day	17	7/8	5, 8
		Up says he's looking after Tech's crib.				

One Liner

ABC/FTP PRODUCTIONS, LLC
CALL SHEET

"PILOT"

EXEC PRODUCERS:	BERT SALKE, CHRIS BRANCATO
EXEC. PRDO/WRITER:	JESSICA GOLDSTEIN
CONSULTING PROD/CO-CREATOR:	HAMISH LINKLATER
PRODUCER:	JUSTIN GREENE
ASSOC. PRODUCER:	HEATHER MEEHAN, MARC KAHN
EXEC. PRDO/DIRECTOR:	JACK BENDER

ABC STUDIOS
500 S. BUENA VISTA STREET BURBANK, CA 91521
PHONE

MICH#
100 R.
DETR#
PHO!

LEAVE: 1:48P
CREW CALL: 2P

DAY/DATE: Wednesday, July 16, 2008

DAY 14	OF	14
SHOOTING CALL	2:45P
SUNRISE:	6:07A
SUNSET:	9:07P
WEATHER:	86, 20% Chance of Rain
	Ise Thunderstorms starting at 7P
HOSPITAL:	HARPER HOSPITAL
	3990 John R. Road
	Detroit, MI
	313/745-

DISTANT LOCATION TRAVEL TIME IS FROM MARRIOTT ~12 MINUTES

#	SET & SCENE DESCRIPTION	D/N	CAST	PGS.	LOCATION
A5PT.1	INT. JAMIE'S APARTMENT	N1	1	6/8	1560 HOWARD STREET
	Jamie packing watching the news				DETROIT
B6	INT. JAMIE'S APARTMENT	N1	1	1/8	
	Jamie tries to sleep				LOC #1CREW PARKING:
C5PT.1	INT. JAMIE'S APARTMENT	N1	1	1/8	FAIRDALE 1401 ROSA PARKS BLVD
	Jamie wakes up looks out/sees man in truck outside				BASECAMP/WORKING TRUCKS &
					CATERING @ STAGE
INSERTS TO SHOOT @ WAREHOUSE					
41PT.	INT. BATHROOM-ADDITIONAL COVERAGE	D2	1PD	1/8	
	Letter floating in clear tub of water				
5PT.	INT. CLASSROOM	D1	1PD	-	
	Jamie POV of cell phone-27 missed calls, "Dad"				
61PT,63PT,	INT. ND LOCATION	D4	-		
65PT,67PT	Typewriter keys hit paper				
26PT.	INT. EAST FOUNDRY	D1	1PD	-	
	Jamie's POV of oil on his hands				
25PT.	INT. EAST FOUNDRY	D1	-	-	
	Jamie's POV of radio inside hero truck				
54pt.	EXT. CEMETERY	D3	6PD	-	FX EXPLOSION
	Peels POV of letter, grass in BG				TEST AT 1PM W/ FIRE SAFETY OFFICER
	******MOVE ACROSS STREET***********				
44PT.2	INT. HAMILTON DINING ROOM/EXPLOSION	N2	-	1/8	
	Insert elements, Dad blows up/wall blows				
	******INSERT CAR WORK***********				
55PT.	EXT. MUSCLE CAR-TRAVELING	D3	1,ATMO	1/8	24TH & MICHIGAN TO ROSA PARKS
	Jamie traveling after his run in with Mom				
	COMPANY MOVE TO DOWNTOWN/LOAD IN @ TIMES SQUARE MAINTENANCE FACILITY				
59	INT. PEOPLE MOVER	N4	1,9,24,ATMO	3/8	BRICKTOWN PEOPLE MOVER STOP
	Jamie talks with the Bum/Ghost				
58	EXT. PEOPLE MOVER	N4	1,8,24,ATMO	1 3/8	
	Train stop/Chris doesn't make it on/Jamie pulls away				
			TOTAL	3 1/8	

CAST	STATUS	CHARACTER	CRTSY PU	CALL	SET	SPECIAL INSTRUCTIONS, MISC.
1. WARREN	WF	Jamie Hamilton	1:50P	2P	2:45P	
3. PIPER	TR	Meg Garnet		TRAVEL		
8. BENNY	WF	Chris Ramirez		W/IN @ 8P		
9. RUTGER	WF	James Hamilton III	7:50P	8P	9P	BRING TO BASECAMP #2
13. HUDSON (X)	TR	Young Jamie		TRAVEL		
24. FRANK	SWF	Bum	7:40P	8P	9P	PU @ RM, BRING TO BASECAMP #2
X TOM	TR	Stunt Coordinator		TRAVEL		
X1 TOBIASZ	TR	Jamie Double		TRAVEL		
X3 ALICIA	TR	Meg Double		TRAVEL		

ALL CALLS SUBJECT TO CHANGE AT WRAP BY UPM OR AD'S. NO WEEKEND WORK, FORCED CALLS or NPV'S WITHOUT PRIOR APPROVAL BY UPM. SAFETY MEETINGS @ CALL
BY FIRST AD ON FIRST DAY OF EPISODE, ON FIRST DAY AT NEW LOCATION, WHENEVER STUNTS, SPECIAL EFFECTS, OR UNUSUAL ACTIVITY IS SCHEDULED.

STAND INS & ATMOSPHERE	RPT @	DEPARTMENTAL NOTES	
REPORT TO CREW PARKING #1		PROPS:	Sc. A5: Suitcase,clothes; Sc. 44: Hero envelope;
Stallen (Jamie & photo double)	2P		Sc. 44: Dust masks, eye protection available; Sc. 58: Chris's bottles to break
PAUL PHOTO DOUBLE	2P		Inserts: Hero typewriter, Jamie's cell, Paul's hero letter
Report to Crew Parking #1		SET DRESSING:	Practical TV, matching bathroom set; Sc. 44; Turner Landscape, Wall units
Sc. 44:			Inserts: Grey table top, Desk for Typewriter
2 ND Drivers w/ cars	3P	HAIR/MU:	Sc. C6: Possible cuts on Jamie
		FX:	Jamie: Rain, wind, breakaway windows x3; Bathroom: Blood drips into water;
REPORT TO BASECAMP#2			Sc. 44: explosion, air mortars; atmo smoke in People mover
REPORT TO BASECAMP#2		VIDEO PLAYBACK:	Sc. A6: Green loop on TV; Sc. C6: TV crackles on; Ab switcher
Jim (James), Michael (Chris/Bum)	9P	OPTICAL FX:	Sc. 44: Explosion elements; INSERTS: Jamie cell phone burn in, macro lens for typewriter
		SPECIAL EQUIPMENT:	AB Switcher, 90'Condor, 110' Condor
		GRIP/ELECTRIC:	Sc. 44: Green screen
		POST PRODUCTION:	Reference video for inserts
		ADDL. LABOR:	Video Playback @ 1:30P, Fire Safety Officer, 2 PA's, C Camera Op & 1st AC
		TRANSPO:	Sc. 55: Muscle Car, Insert Car w/ process trailer @ 3P
			Adler Pickups above, Crew pickups on back
		LOCATIONS:	ITC,Load in area at Times Square Maintenance, Fire Safety @ 4P for Explosion set
			Restroom trailer @ Insert Car location
TOTAL COUNT:	2		Inserts: Hero Truck from Foundry inside Stage

SCENES	SET & SCENE DESCRIPTION	D/N	CAST	PGS.	LOCATION
ADVANCE SHOOTING SCHEDULE					

**THANK YOU TO OUR HARD WORKING CAST & CREW
FOR A GREAT SHOOT!**

Thank You!

| UPM: MARY COURTNEY | 1st AD: RICHARD SCHROER | Key 2nd AD: CARLA BOWEN | 2nd 2nd: NORMAN KALI |
| VP PRODUCTION: JIM GASTON | | 313/949- | 313/919- |

Sides (Front Page)

Prince of Motor City - 'Pilot' - FULL GOLD - 6/29/08   3.

INT. CLASSROOM - DAY   ⑤

Jamie continues his lecture, behind him on the blackboard the
class title: "Atheism, Theism, Existentialism".

                    JAMIE
        Well the flat fact is: dead is
        dead. There are no princes,
        princesses, no magic kisses,   *
        there's no Yoda, no force, no   *
        turning back time. There is only
        this life, and what you choose to
        do with it. Only this life...   *

Jamie stops for a moment as if lost in those words. The class *
watches him concerned.   *

                    STUDENT   *
        Mr. Hamilton?   *

Jamie's snaps to-   *

                    JAMIE   *
        Okay, okay that's it for today, but   *
        for next week I suggest you *choose*   *
        to hit your Nietzsche like he's   *
        going out of style.   *

The class LAUGHS, starts to get up, JAMIE turns on his CELL,   *
He checks it, 27 MISSED CALLS! It immediately RINGS. He   *
answers it, we hear Elvis' smooth voice through it singing,
MY BOY.

                    JAMIE (CONT'D)   *
        Listen, I don't know who you are
        but stop messing with me.

He hangs up the phone. ANNA THAYER, his TA, looks over at   *
him concerned.

                    ANNA
        You okay?   *

                    JAMIE
        Yeah, crank calls.   *

He turns off his phone.   *

                    ANNA   *
        Another coed stalking the cute   *
        Professor.   *

He smiles, she starts to walk away, then...   *

Sides (Script Page)

Mark Adler

CALL SHEET						CALL SHEET			

DAY/DATE: 25-Sep-08 **Job/Product:** **Sunrise:** 7:20 am
Day : Thursday 2 of 2 **Job #:** 805 **Sunset:** 7:28pm **CREW CALL:**

PRODUCTION COMPANY: PHONE : FAX :

ADVERTISING AGENCY : PHONE : FAX :

PROD. CELL : **Location Info:** Ann Arbor, Mi **CREW PARKING:**

CREW	NAME	PHONE	DAYS	IN	OUT	TOTAL	NOTES & SPECIAL EQUIPMENT:
Director	J.B.			7:30a	6:30p		
DP	Barry			7:30a	6:30p		
Executive Producer	Ed			o/c			
Producer	Bruce			o/c			
1st AD	Zak			7:30a	6:30p		
Production Supervis	Diane			7:30a	7:30p		
1st Assist Camera	Dave			7:30a	6:30p		
Gaffer	Darry			7:30a	6:30p		
Best Boy Electric							
3rd Electric							
Key Grip	Mark			7:30a	6:30p		
Audio Mixer	J.E			7:30a	3p		
Wardrobe	Stacy			7:30a	5p		
Script / MU	Carolyn			7:30a	5p		
Production Assist	Curt			7:30a	7:30p		
Production Assist	Alicia			7:30a	7:30p		
Craft Services	Craig			7:30a	6:30p		
Location Scout	Tom			7:30a	7:30p		
Moho driver	Jerry			7:30a	7:30p		

EQUIPMENT	VENDOR	PHONE
CAMERA	Camera Partner	
CAR SERVICE		
LIGHTING	Mad Dog	
CATERER		
CRANE - TECHN		
CAMERA CAR		
CAR PREP		
CONDOR		
CG	UI	
EDITORIAL		
HOTEL-director		
HOTEL-talent		
GRIP & GENNIE	Mad Dog	
INSURANCE	Albert G. Ruber	
LABORATORY		
MOTORHOME	CampRCruise	
PAYROLL	Olympic Partner	
PASS VAN		
RAW STOCK		
TABLES/CHAIR		
TRUCKING		
WALKIES	Camera Partner	
WATER TRUCK		
VIDEO ASST		

TALENT ROLE	TALENT NAME	PHONE	ALTERNATE	IN	OUT	TOTAL	AGENT	PHONE	CONTACT
Anchor Lifter	Adam Southall			8a	4p		iGroup Talent		Tony
Anchor Lifter	Joseph Smith			8a	4p				
Photographer	Max Lund			8a	4p				
Anchor Watcher	Chantaya Bryant			8a	4p				
Anchor Watcher	Jovan LaRocque			8a	4p				
Student	Carmen Calhoun			8a	5:30p				
Student	Kojo Asadoo			8a	5:30p				
Student	Matt Lund			8a	4p				
Student	Camarelli			8a	4p				

PRODUCTION SUMMARY		FILM STOCK & AUDIO	
First Shot AM:	8:30a	STOCK #	
Lunch	2-2:30p	AMOUNT ON HAND	
First Shot PM:	2:35p	SHOT TODAY	
Dinner		SHOT TO DATE	
First Shot PM:		REMAINING UNEXPOSED	
Wrap Pix	6p	REMAINING SHORT ENDS	
Wrap Production	6:30p	TOTAL ON HAND	
		AUDIO ROLLS ON HAND	

PRODUCTION NOTES:

Revised 9/28/2008, 9:56 PM

Call sheet

67

WALKIE-TALKIE SIGN-OUT SHEET

DATE RECEIVED FROM VENDOR	P.O. NUMBER	ITEM(S) & MODEL NO INCLUDING ACCESSORIES	SERIAL NUMBER	UNIT NUMBER	DEPARTMENT ASSIGNED TO	PRINT NAME	DATE OUT	DATE IN	SIGNATURE	DATE RETURNED TO VENDOR

VENDOR

ADDRESS

VENDOR

ADDRESS

PHONE NUMBER (   )   -

CONTACT

NOTES

Film Production Company

OMB No. 1615-0047; Expires 06/30/08

Department of Homeland Security
U.S. Citizenship and Immigration Services

Form I-9, Employment Eligibility Verification

Please read instructions carefully before completing this form. The instructions must be available during completion of this form.

ANTI-DISCRIMINATION NOTICE: It is illegal to discriminate against work eligible individuals. Employers CANNOT specify which document(s) they will accept from an employee. The refusal to hire an individual because the documents have a future expiration date may also constitute illegal discrimination.

Section 1. Employee Information and Verification. To be completed and signed by employee at the time employment begins.

Print Name: Last	First	Middle Initial	Maiden Name
Address (Street Name and Number)		Apt. #	Date of Birth (month/day/year)
City	State	Zip Code	Social Security #

I am aware that federal law provides for imprisonment and/or fines for false statements or use of false documents in connection with the completion of this form.	I attest, under penalty of perjury, that I am (check one of the following): ☐ A citizen or national of the United States ☐ A lawful permanent resident (Alien # A ☐ An alien authorized to work until (Alien # or Admission #)

Employee's Signature	Date (month/day/year)

Preparer and/or Translator Certification. *(To be completed and signed if Section 1 is prepared by a person other than the employee.) I attest, under penalty of perjury, that I have assisted in the completion of this form and that to the best of my knowledge the information is true and correct.*

Preparer's/Translator's Signature	Print Name
Address (Street Name and Number, City, State, Zip Code)	Date (month/day/year)

Section 2. Employer Review and Verification. To be completed and signed by employer. Examine one document from List A OR examine one document from List B and one from List C, as listed on the reverse of this form, and record the title, number and expiration date, if any, of the document(s).

List A	OR	List B	AND	List C
Document title:				
Issuing authority:				
Document #:				
Expiration Date (if any):				
Document #:				
Expiration Date (if any):				

CERTIFICATION - I attest, under penalty of perjury, that I have examined the document(s) presented by the above-named employee, that the above-listed document(s) appear to be genuine and to relate to the employee named, that the employee began employment on (month/day/year) _____ and that to the best of my knowledge the employee is eligible to work in the United States. (State employment agencies may omit the date the employee began employment.)

Signature of Employer or Authorized Representative	Print Name	Title
Business or Organization Name and Address (Street Name and Number, City, State, Zip Code)		Date (month/day/year)

Section 3. Updating and Reverification. To be completed and signed by employer.

A. New Name (if applicable)	B. Date of Rehire (month/day/year) (if applicable)

C. If employee's previous grant of work authorization has expired, provide the information below for the document that establishes current employment eligibility.

Document Title:	Document #:	Expiration Date (if any):

I attest, under penalty of perjury, that to the best of my knowledge, this employee is eligible to work in the United States, and if the employee presented document(s), the document(s) I have examined appear to be genuine and to relate to the individual.

Signature of Employer or Authorized Representative	Date (month/day/year)

Sample Time Card with I9.

Jared Production Services
"I'm the glue holding the show together"

1234 Main St
Lansing, MI 48xxx
Phone 517.555.1555 Fax 517.555.2555
Email: JPS@gmail.com

INVOICE

INVOICE #[100]
DATE JAN 13 20XX

TO:
The Show
4055 Vine
Hollywood CA 90xxx
323.555.5555
Att: Payroll

FOR:
THE SHOW
Job#:
P.O. Number:

DESCRIPTION	HOURS	RATE	AMOUNT
Production Services as Production Assistant Week of Jan, 7 – Jan 12 20xx	13 hours *flat*	$125/day	$625
		TOTAL	$625.00

Make all checks payable to Jared Production Services
Total due in 15 days. Overdue accounts subject to a service charge of 1% per month.

Thank you for your business!

Production Credits

Lauren Jareds

Office 248.349.xxxx Mobile 248.797.xxxx
Internet: Ljareds@prodmail.com

--Production Assistant --

FEATURE FILMS: (SELECT CREDITS 20xx)

Madhouse, Director: Tony Windman   (Key Set P.A.)
Producer: Andrew Man   Locations in SE Michigan

The City, Director: John Berg   (Production Assistant)
Producer: Wayne Holder   Howell MI

I Want That, Director: Scott Olik   (Locations P.A.)
Producer: Scooter Singer   Livonia, MI

EDUCATION: Bachelor of Arts, Telecommunications, University of Michigan 20xx

Production Mileage Report

Name:_____ **Project Title**: _____

Department: _____ **Week ending**: _____

Date	Purpose of Trip	Start Miles	End Miles	Total

Mark Adler

PETTY CASH SUMMARY

Employee Name	Employee Phone No.	Job Name	Category	Envelope No.
		Job No.		Of:

Date	Rec't No.	To Whom	For What	Amount																	

TOTALS
TOTAL DISBURSED
AMOUNT RECEIVED
BAL DUE EMPLOYEE
BALANCE DUE

Employee Signature

No payment for services rendered will be
made until petty cash is cleared by produx

ENTERPRISE PRINTERS & STATIONERS 7401 SUNSET BLVD LOS ANGELES 90046 (213)876-3531 FAX (213)876-4398 184A

73

PETTY CASH ENVELOPE

Name:
Position:
Picture:

Date:
Check No:
Check/Cash Received:
RECEIVED BY:

UPM:
Audit:
Show #

Prod'n:
Dept:
TRANS #
VENDOR #
VOUCHER #

DATE	TO WHOM PAID	PURPOSE	ACCOUNTING USE ONLY				
			SET NUMBER	INV ITEM #	NET AMOUNT *BEFORE GST*	GST AMOUNT	TOTAL RECEIPT
1							
2							
3							
4							
5							
6							
7							
8							
9							
10							
11							
12							
13							
14							
15							
16							
17							
18							
19							
20							

TOTAL RECEIPTS

* SUMMARY-FOR ACCOUNTING ONLY *

ACCOUNT NUMBER	AMOUNT	DESCRIPTION	ACCOUNT NUMBER	AMOUNT	DESCRIPTION

* Net Amount is to include Provincial Sales Tax

ABOUT THE AUTHOR

ABOUT THE AUTHOR

Photo by Elayne Gross

During the past twenty years, Mark Adler has developed his creative and organizational skills in positions ranging from Trainer and Director to Producer and President of VAIdigital LLC, a video support company for the film industry. At present, Mark divides his time between managing VAIdigital, video support for filmmakers, and building his 501c6 trade organization, the Michigan Production Alliance, with the goal of creating a more stable financial environment for the production community in Michigan. During his career, Mark has trained hundreds of individuals in the use of production and multimedia methods and technology. As President and primary technician of VAIdigital, Mark functions as liaison and consultant on the aspects of commercial and feature film productions, as well as providing rental of video assist and TelePrompTer display systems.

VAIdigital has provided service on local, regional, and national commercials, as well as feature films such as Innocence Production's *Betty Anne Waters,* Duke of York's *All's Faire in Love,* Parallel Media's *High School,* the HD feature *Crossover* for 360 Films, Paramount Pictures' *Hardball,* Paramount's *Four Brothers,* and Universal/Imagine Entertainment's *8 Mile, Celebrate Detroit* (an IMAX film), *Hoffa,* and *Rosary Murders,* as well as operating teleprompters for city officials and executives of major international corporations.

Prior to broadcast work, Mark was responsible for the design, oversight, and implementation of MacLean-Hunter Cable LTD's community access center in EastPointe and Centerline, Michigan. As Production Manager, his skills were tested in all areas from budget management, training staff, officials, and volunteers to lighting, editing, camera operating, and directing.

Mark quite literally built a production facility, a mobile production vehicle, and a following of community volunteers in order to create entertainment and informational programming for the franchise area. With the startup complete, Mark moved into commercial production in 1982.

EDUCATION

Bachelor of Arts, Telecommunications, Political Science, Michigan State University, East Lansing, MI

Journalism, Mass Media Studies, Wayne State University, Detroit, MI

PROFESSIONAL AFFILIATIONS

Michigan Production Alliance—Director, co-founder/President

Michigan Media Professionals—former board member, programming committee member

Novi Cable Access Committee—former member/chair, twelve years of service

IATSE—Local 812 Studio Mechanics member since 1986

Art Institute of Michigan—Advisory Committee member

For more information about Mark Adler, please visit www.mpami.org, www.vaidigital.com, and the Michigan Production Alliance group page on www.facebook.com